DeltaScienceReaders™

Butterflies and Moths

CONTENTS

Think About . . .

What Are Living Things? 2

What Is an Insect? 4

Butterflies and Moths 6

Life Cycle of Butterflies and Moths 8

Egg 9

Larva 10

Pupa 11

Adult 12

Other Insect Life Cycles 13

People in Science

A Biologist 14

Did You Know?

About Migration 15

Glossary 16

What Are Living Things?

How are a tree, an elephant, and a butterfly alike? They are all living things. All plants and animals are living things. **Living things** can grow and change. Things that are not alive are called **nonliving things.** Rocks, water, and air are nonliving things.

Plants and animals need different things to stay alive. Plants need air, water, and light. Plants also need nutrients. **Nutrients** are nonliving things that plants get from soil. Animals need air, water, and food. Most animals also need shelter, a place to live.

A tree, an elephant, and a butterfly look very different. Yet they are all living things.

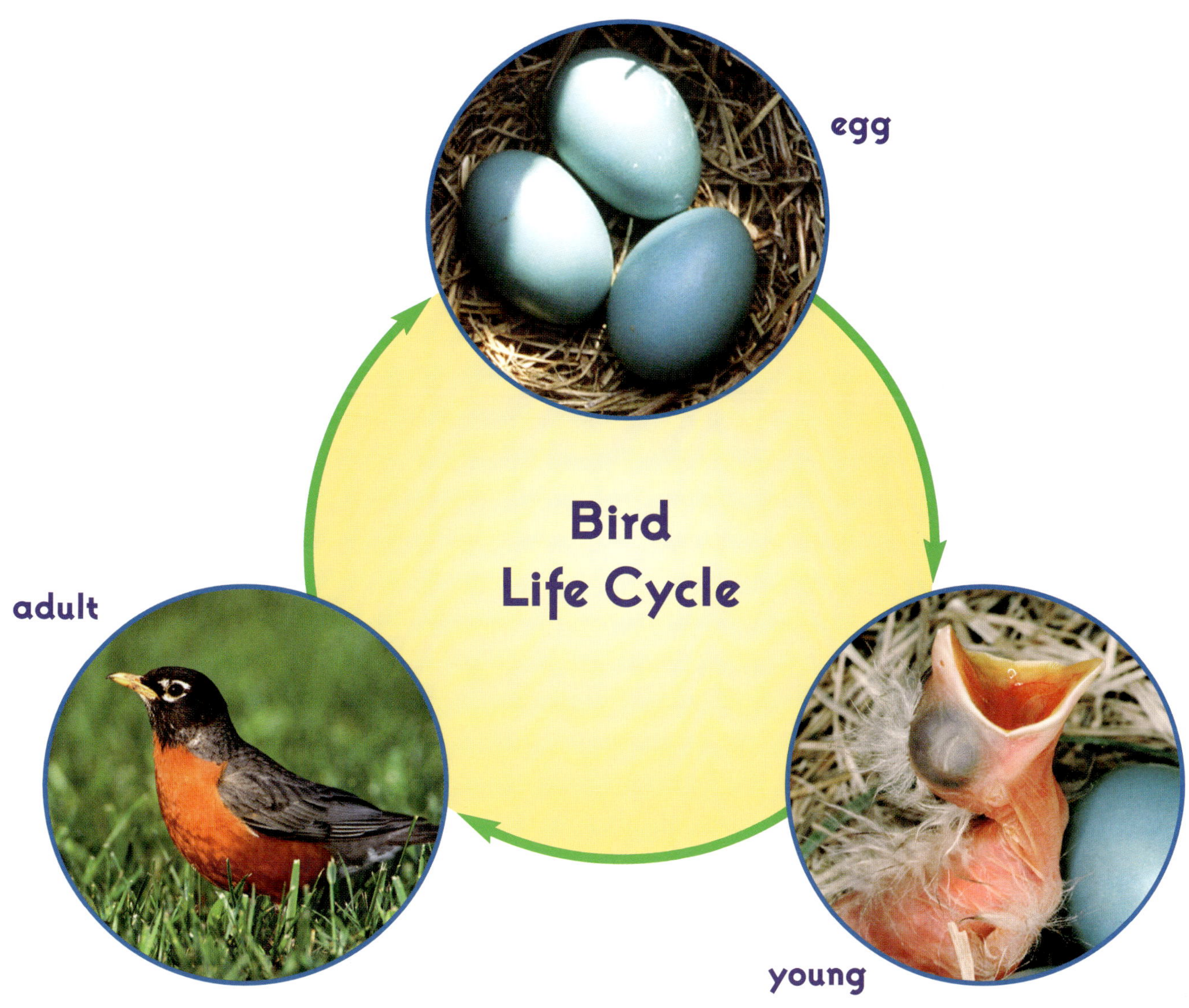

Living things change as they grow. A plant grows from a seed. A bird grows from an egg. All the steps in a plant or an animal's life are called a **life cycle.**

A grown-up animal is called an **adult.** Some young animals look a lot like adults. Some do not. A kitten looks like a small cat. But a tadpole looks very different from an adult frog.

What Is an Insect?

More than half the animals on Earth are **insects.** There are more than one million different kinds of insects. Scientists group plants and animals by how they look and how they live. Insects are one group of animals.

Butterflies and moths are insects. Bees, ants, beetles, and grasshoppers are insects, too. Insects have three main body parts. These are called the **head,** the **thorax,** and the **abdomen.** Insects have six legs. Most insects have wings. Most insects have **antennae,** or feelers, on their heads, too. Insects have an exoskeleton. An **exoskeleton** is a hard covering that protects the body.

Insects live almost everywhere on Earth. They live on cold, snowy mountains. They live in hot deserts. Some insects even live on water.

Some beetles live in deserts, rain forests, or lakes. Some live on the tops of mountains.

Water striders are also called pond skaters. They can move across the surface of the water.

Ladybug

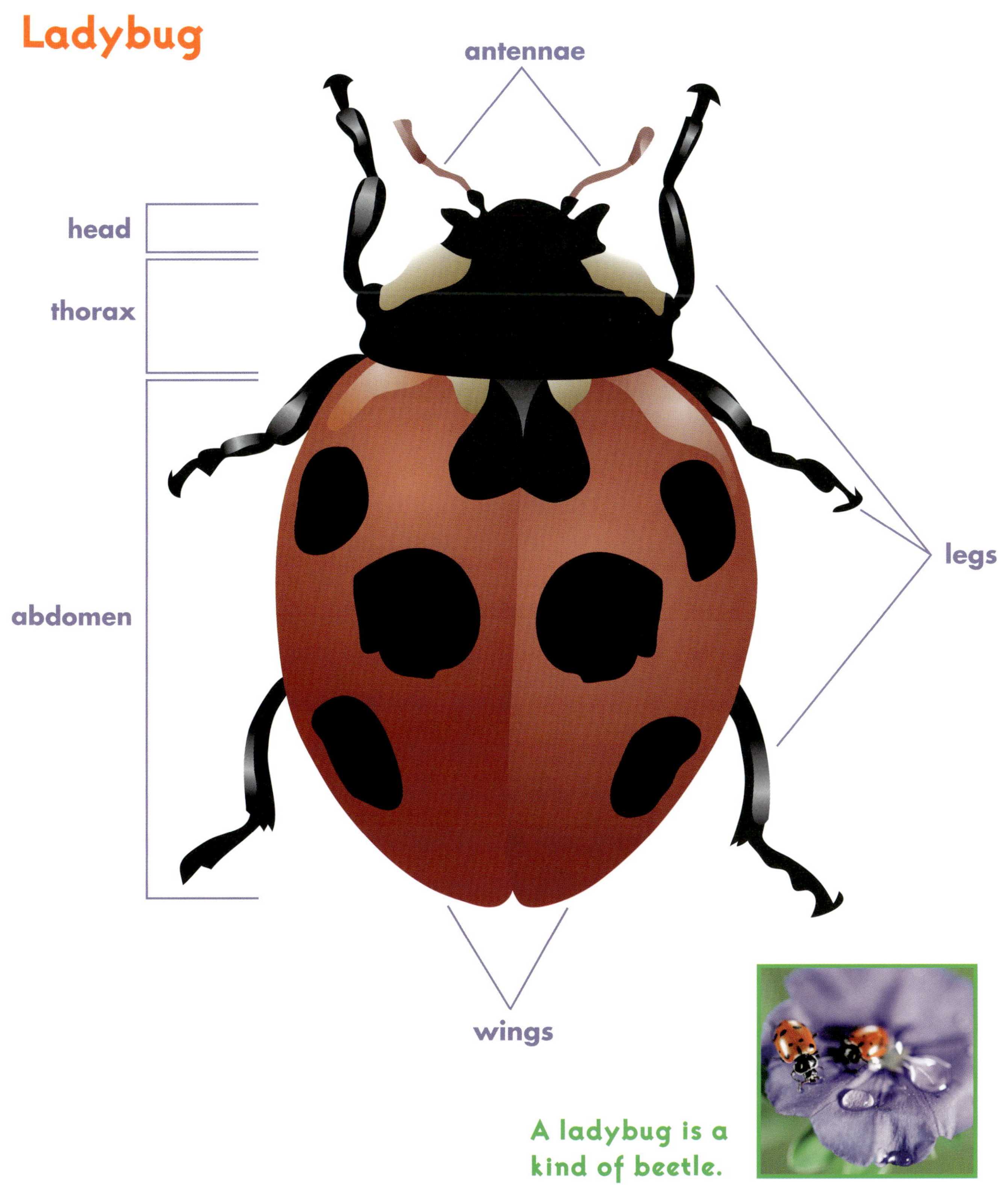

A ladybug is a kind of beetle.

Butterflies and Moths

A poet called butterflies "flowers that fly." Their bright colors come from fuzzy scales on their wings. The scales overlap, like shingles on a roof. Look for butterflies in gardens or in fields during the day. Butterflies rest with their wings folded together.

Most moths fly at night. Look for them fluttering around lights. Most moths are brown or pale in color. But some are bright. Moths rest with their wings spread out.

Butterflies and moths are alike in many ways. They both have scales on their wings. They both lay eggs. Their life cycles have the same stages. Some butterflies and moths even look alike.

Butterflies and moths are different in some ways, too. Most moths are smaller than butterflies. Moths are often less colorful.

There are more than 160,000 kinds of butterflies and moths. Some are as small as this letter *O*. Some are bigger than both your hands held side by side.

Life Cycle of Butterflies and Moths

Butterflies and moths have a life cycle with four steps, or stages. First an adult lays an **egg.** A few days or weeks go by. Then the egg hatches.

A **larva** comes out of the egg. The larva is also called a caterpillar. A larva eats and grows. Then it forms a covering around itself. Now it is called a **pupa.**

The pupa changes. It sheds its covering. It is now an adult butterfly or moth. This change in form from egg to adult is called **metamorphosis.**

The word for more than one larva is *larvae.* The word for more than one pupa is *pupae.*

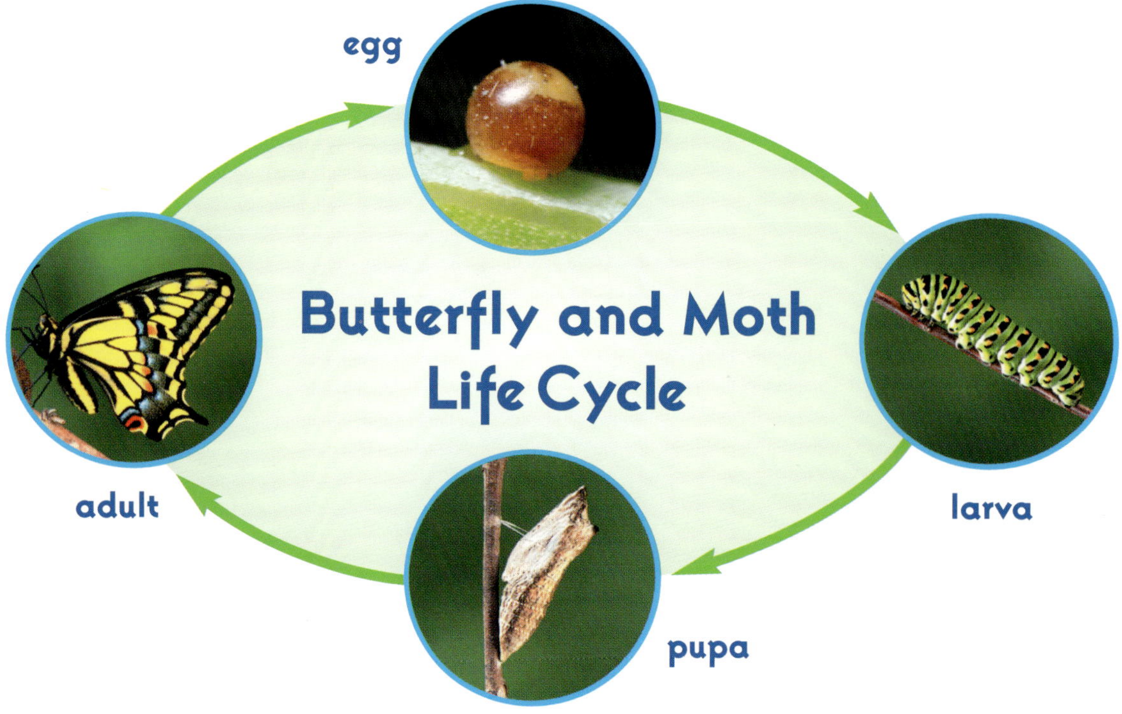

Egg

The eggs of butterflies and moths are very tiny. Each egg is about the size of a grain of salt. Some eggs are laid in clumps. Some are laid one by one.

The place where butterflies and moths lay their eggs is very important. The eggs have to be laid on just the right plant. The plant will be food for the larvae. Eggs can dry out in the sun. They can wash away in rain. Insect eggs can be food for other animals, too. Birds, lizards, and spiders eat insect eggs.

A safe place for eggs is underneath a leaf. Still, very few eggs will grow into adults.

A butterfly may lay eggs on a milkweed plant.

butterfly eggs

moth eggs

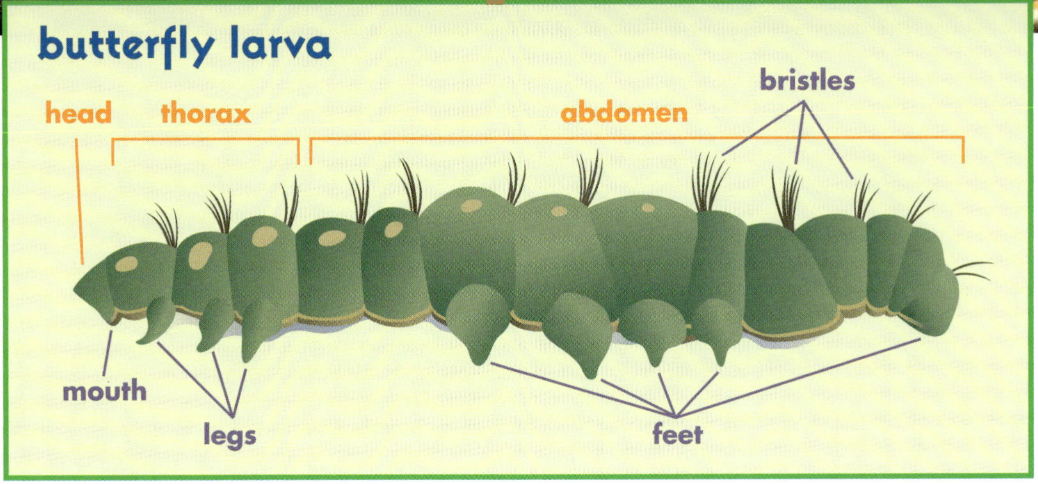

Larva

Most eggs hatch into larvae in three to ten days. Larvae have long bodies with three main parts. They have exoskeletons. They have six legs on their thorax. Larvae also have short feet on their abdomen. Larvae can bend and crawl.

Larvae are always eating. First they eat the shells of their eggs. Then they eat the leaves around them. As a larva eats, it grows. Soon it outgrows its stiff exoskeleton. The larva sheds this skin. New skin is underneath. The new skin gets hard. It forms a new exoskeleton. This happens many times as a larva grows.

Some butterfly larvae eat milkweed plants.

Pupa

Next comes the biggest change. Each larva forms a covering around itself. Now it is a pupa.

A butterfly pupa is smooth. Some pupae have little gold spots on them. They hang from leaves or twigs. A butterfly pupa is also called a **chrysalis.**

A moth pupa looks like a white web. Moth pupae can be found in hidden places. Some are tucked under tree bark. Others are in folded leaves. A moth pupa is also called a **cocoon.**

The pupa stage lasts for a week or two. Then the pupa sheds its covering. The insect is now an adult.

butterfly chrysalis

moth cocoon

Adult

The flying moths and butterflies that we see are adult insects. They have stopped growing. Most of them live only a short time. Some live a few days. Others live a few months.

Some butterflies and moths eat nectar. **Nectar** is the sweet liquid found in flowers. Other butterflies and moths eat tree sap or the juice from fruit. A few adult butterflies and moths do not eat at all.

Adult female butterflies and moths lay eggs. An egg hatches into a larva. The life cycle continues.

A butterfly gets nectar from a flower with its long mouthpiece. It is called a proboscis.

Other Insect Life Cycles

Butterflies and moths have a life cycle with four stages. So do ants, bees, flies, and beetles. These insects change shape as they grow.

Other insects do not change shape. They have a life cycle with three stages. The stages are egg, nymph, and adult.

Nymphs hatch from eggs. Nymphs look like small adults. They eat and grow. They shed their skins, just as larvae do. Crickets, grasshoppers, and dragonflies grow in this way.

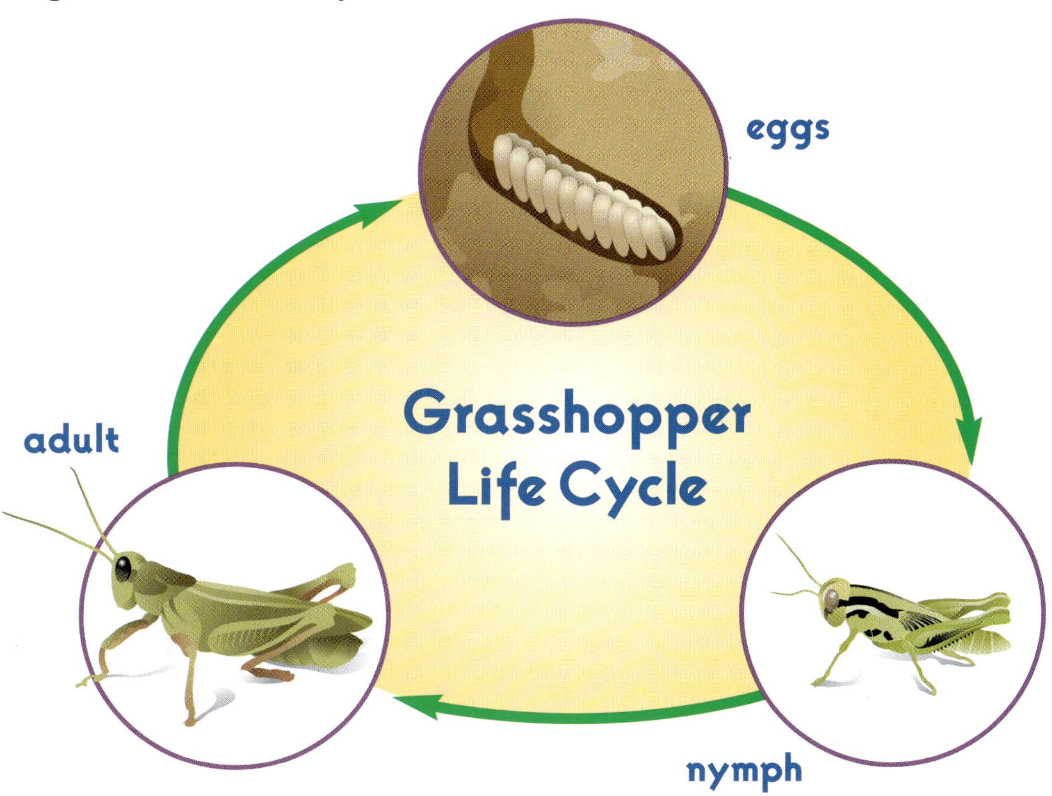

A Biologist

How does it feel to have a butterfly walk on your head? Dr. Karen Oberhauser knows. She has been studying Monarch butterflies for 20 years. She is a biologist. A biologist is a scientist who studies living things.

Dr. Oberhauser studies the life cycle of Monarch butterflies. She also studies where Monarchs live. People all over the United States send her the information she needs. She also shows teachers how to study butterflies in their classrooms.

Years ago, Dr. Oberhauser went to Mexico to see the Monarchs' winter home for the first time. She says that it was a big day in her life. Since then, she has visited the butterflies there many times.

Monarchs huddle on trees all winter.

Did You Know?

About Migration

Monarch butterflies fly south for the winter! Most of the Monarchs fly to warmer weather in California or Mexico. Some of them fly 3,200 kilometers (about 2,000 miles)! Millions of Monarchs make the trip. This kind of travel is called **migration.** Some birds, whales, and sea turtles also migrate.

Monarchs gather in trees in winter. This helps them keep warm. When spring comes, they start north. On the way some lay eggs. Few adult butterflies make it all the way back to their summer home. But when the eggs hatch, the new butterflies go the rest of the way north. They will migrate south the next fall.

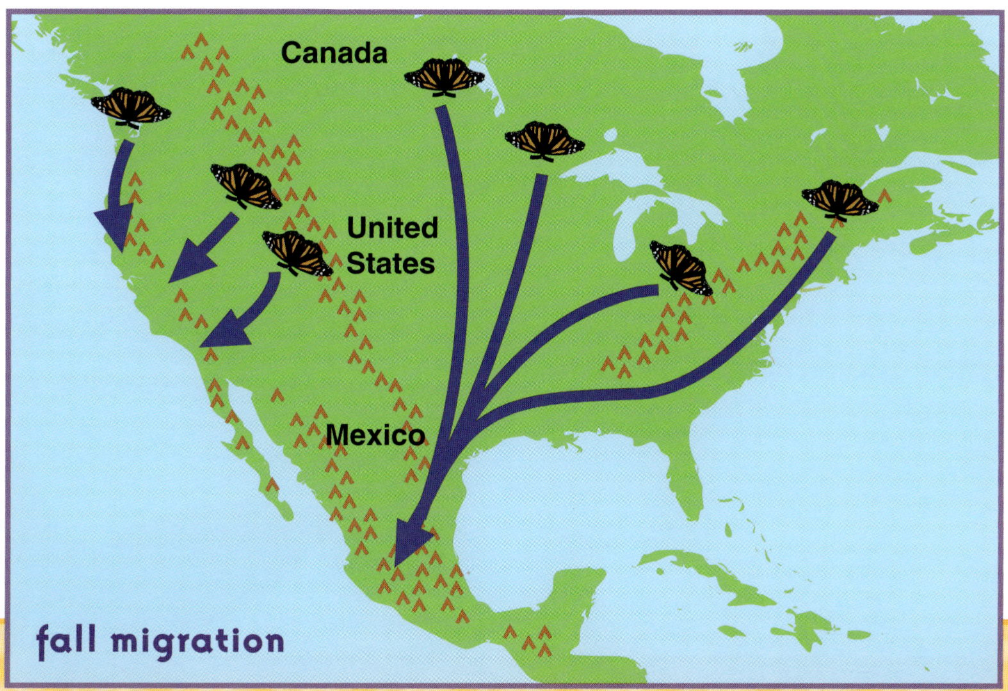

fall migration

Glossary

abdomen one of the three main parts of an insect's body

adult grown plant or animal

antenna feeler on an insect's head used for feeling, tasting, and smelling (plural, *antennae*)

chrysalis pupa of a butterfly

cocoon pupa of a moth

egg first stage in the life cycle of an insect

exoskeleton hard outer covering on an insect's body

head one of the three main parts of an insect's body

insects animals with three main body parts, six legs, and an exoskeleton

larva young insect between the egg and pupa stage (plural, *larvae)*; also called *caterpillar*

life cycle all the changes a plant or an animal goes through during its life

living things plants and animals that can grow and change

metamorphosis complete change in form during the life cycle

migration travel by a group of animals from one area to another, often over long distances

nectar sweet liquid in flowers

nonliving things things that are not alive, such as rocks, water, and air

nutrients nonliving things that plants get from soil to help them grow

nymph young insect that looks like a small adult; the nymph stage is the second stage of a life cycle that has three stages

pupa young insect between the larva and adult stage (plural, *pupae)*

thorax one of the three main parts of an insect's body